The Sneaky Freckle

Dana Rodriguez

To Sophia, whose beautiful heart is as big as her dreams.

To my Dad, who always knew the next adventure was just around the corner.

Sophie was a beautiful little girl with big green eyes and perfectly rosy cheeks.

One morning, as Sophie was in her room getting ready for the day, she noticed something very different about herself. Staring intently at her reflection, Sophie discovered a mark she hadn't seen before. Directly under her left eye, on her perfectly rosy cheek, was a small brown spot.

Within a few days, there were even more small brown spots scattered across her beautiful face.

The following week, Sophie visited a dermatologist. A dermatologist is a doctor who treats different types of skin issues, ranging from rashes to wrinkles.

The dermatologist let Sophie know that the spots on her face weren't caused by a rash. They were *freckles*! The dermatologist also explained that freckles are harmless, so there was no need for Sophie to be concerned.

Freckles continued popping up on Sophie's face until there was a cluster of small brown spots crossing over her tiny nose as they stretched from one cheek to the other. Sophie couldn't believe what was happening. Every day, there seemed to be a new freckle...or two!

Sophie was completely frustrated by those sneaky freckles. It was obvious they were spreading, and she was desperate to get rid of them... even if they were *harmless*.

She tried peeling them off.

She tried rubbing them off.

She even tried washing them off with warm, soapy water.

Despite Sophie's best efforts to remove the small brown spots, they remained on her perfectly rosy cheeks.

Sophie felt totally defeated. Then, an idea came to her. If she couldn't

remove the small brown spots, perhaps she could hide them instead.

Rummaging through her parents' bedroom in search of a solution, Sophie stumbled upon her Mom's makeup bag. Applying various shades of eyeshadow and blush to her face, Sophie attempted to disguise the small brown spots. Unfortunately, she used way too much makeup, which only made the freckles more obvious.

Next, Sophie wandered to the bathroom in search of a solution. Cautiously climbing to the top of the sink, she took several band-aids from the medicine cabinet and carefully unwrapped each one. Looking closely in the mirror, Sophie tried to conceal the small brown spots by placing different sized band-aids across her face. Unfortunately, she used way too many band-aids, which only made the freckles more obvious.

Finally, Sophie darted to the basement in search of a solution. Digging through the dusty boxes and bags that were scattered throughout the darkened room, she spotted an oversized beach bag hanging on the wall. At the very bottom of the canvas tote, Sophie found her Mom's favorite sun hat. Sophie tried to cover up the small brown spots as she gently placed the wide-brimmed hat on top of her head. Unfortunately, the hat was way too big. It hid the freckles... and Sophie!

Later that night, as Sophie was getting ready for bed, she took a long look at herself in the bathroom mirror. She suddenly realized she had put those sneaky freckles through an awful lot. Standing there without makeup, band-aids, or a wide-brimmed hat, those small brown spots didn't seem so bad.

Sophie had an unexpected change of heart. Rather than hide her small brown spots, now she wants to flaunt them. Just as each freckle is unique, Sophie truly has a look that's as unique as she is.

In spite of everything, Sophie has finally come to love her look as much as she loves her...sneaky freckles.

About the Author

Dana was born and raised much of her childhood in Germany, which sparked a passion for travel. As a dedicated educator for more than 20 years, Dana taught English & Life Skills to adult immigrants from more than 50 countries, helping them adapt to their new circumstances.

However, Dana's greatest joy comes from being a wife and a mother. With the lessons she learned from these roles, she launched *The Family Journey* website as well as *The Final Thoughts* podcast. Dana is also the author of *The Sneaky Freckle*, with more books to follow in *The Sneaky Series*.

From something as small as a freckle to something as life-altering as a physical handicap, this book series is inspired by the personal challenges her children faced as they were growing up. Dana wrote *The Sneaky Series* as a way to shed light on these issues, while instilling a greater sense of compassion within each of us.

www.ingramcontent.com/pod-product-compliance
Lightning Source LLC
Chambersburg PA
CBHW041501120626
46547CB00003B/502